D. N. RILEY

AERIAL ARCHAEOLOGY IN BRITAIN

SHIRE ARCHAEOLOGY

Cover illustration
Three ring ditches, two of which are incomplete, and probable frost cracks at Edgerly Farm, Clanfield, Oxfordshire. (SP 268020. 23rd July 1972.)

Published by
SHIRE PUBLICATIONS LTD
Cromwell House, Church Street, Princes Risborough,
Aylesbury, Bucks, HP17 9AJ, UK.

Series Editor: James Dyer

ISBN 0 85263 592 3

First published 1982; reprinted 1987.

Set by Avocet, Aylesbury, and printed in Great Britain by
C. I. Thomas & Sons (Haverfordwest) Ltd,
Press Buildings, Merlins Bridge, Haverfordwest.

Contents

Acknowledgements

The photographs are an important part of this book and I am grateful to Jim Pickering for the cover picture, to Chris Stanley for a picture of Silchester (fig. 33), and to the Ashmolean Museum, Oxford, for the photographs by Major G. W. G. Allen (figs. 15, 18, 21, 22 and 25) and for prints of my own early pictures (figs. 3 and 4): the museum preserves the negatives of these photographs and holds the copyright. I also have to acknowledge four photographs supplied by the National Monuments Record Air Photographs Unit (figs. 10, 14, 34 and 39), for which Crown Copyright is reserved. The other photographs, which are my own recent work, have in most cases been enlarged by Peter Morley, who always does a good job. Terry Manby has helped the preparation of the text by supplying information about the site at Thwing.

Finally, I must thank John Collis for reading the text and making helpful suggestions and Dorothy Cruse for typing the fair copy.

List of illustrations

1
Introduction

To the aviator flying above Britain there come into view from time to time wonderfully extensive traces of the work of early man. With the aeroplane to provide a rapidly moving point of vantage and the camera to record what is seen, the archaeologist in the air is in a very advantageous position; he can survey a large area of land in a relatively short time and he has a distant viewpoint, which enables well-known places to be seen in a new way and surprising discoveries to be made about sites which are invisible or barely detectable on the ground.

This book is about the way in which these early remains are recorded from the air, and about what is seen, but it does not attempt to describe the monuments from the point of view of an archaeologist working on the ground, which would open up a large additional range of subjects. It is not easy to summarise the elements of a big subject like aerial archaeology, which has many connections with other disciplines, and the matter included here has been chosen strictly in accordance with its relevance to work from the air, resisting the temptation to digress into the many interesting questions which arise about the archaeology of the sites shown in the illustrations.

The beginnings of archaeological air photography were the result of the impetus given to aviation by the First World War and the increase in the number of fliers at that time. Archaeologists were few then, but among them was one who had been an observer in the Royal Flying Corps, O. G. S. Crawford, who became the most important pioneer of aerial archaeology. Pictures taken on training flights by the Royal Air Force (the new name effective from 1st April 1918) were his first source of information, and they remained important throughout the 1920s. In 1924 he was able to take part in a series of flights over Hampshire, Wiltshire and Dorset, which were financed by A. Keiller, another man with a wartime flying background. Their results were published in the book *Wessex from the Air*, a classic of British – one could say, world – archaeology.

Crawford began to map the aerial discoveries and originated many of the terms still in use at the present day to describe the phenomena seen from the air – shadow sites, soil marks and crop marks – of which more will be said later. His influence was increased by the journal *Antiquity*, which he founded in 1924, and in the pages of this periodical, among other things, he was able to make widely known the photographs taken during the 1930s by Major G. W. G. Allen, a private pilot who made a series of remarkable discoveries, largely near Oxford (for example figs. 21, 22 and 25).

In the summer of 1939, just before the outbreak of the Second World War, Crawford arranged a programme of flights in Scotland in which Dr (later Professor) J. K. St Joseph also took part, though the two men never flew together, because their machine only had room for one person in addition to the pilot. This was the beginning of the work by St Joseph which was later to realise the full potential of archaeological air photography in Britain. Six years later, in 1945, when hostilities were at an end, he began the systematic programme of work which gave rise to the Cambridge University Committee for Aerial Photography. The present author had the very interesting experience of piloting him in the north of England and Scotland in the first few days of his 1945 campaign. From these beginnings the Cambridge University Committee's results have become of the greatest importance, and the air photograph collection, the principal evidence of its success, now totals over 300,000 items. Professor St Joseph has given particular attention to the forts and camps built by the Roman army, but his programme has certainly not been restricted to this, and the whole of Britain and much of Ireland have been examined. Since his recent retirement, the work at Cambridge has been taken over by D. R. Wilson.

In 1965 a second important organisation was formed, the Air Photographs Unit of the National Monuments Record (England). Under the direction of J. N. Hampton, who has done much valuable air photography in recent years (for example, figs. 10, 14 and 39), the Unit has formed a very large archive of photographs, now amounting to about half a million items. The existence of the two great archives in the care of Cambridge University and the National Monuments Record presents a great opportunity and, it may be said, a challenge to archaeologists. The latter collection incorporates the results of various independent pilots, among whom may be mentioned Arnold Baker, John Boyden, Jim Pickering and the present writer. A number of other archaeologists have also begun work in the air in recent years, and the combined efforts of many aviators are making archaeological air survey in Britain a very much more thorough affair than it was in the pioneer days of the 1920s and 1930s.

Although the earliest important archaeological air surveys were made in southern England, and this book only deals with British discoveries, the history of the subject cannot be left without mentioning the independent work begun in the mid 1920s by Père A. Poidebard in Syria, then under French control. His aerial surveys of that region were published in several books, the first of which, *La Trace de Rome dans le Désert de Syrie*, appeared in 1934 and was greeted with enthusiasm by Crawford in the pages of *Antiquity*. Since the Second World War some of the most remarkable results of archaeological air survey have been obtained in France, where Poidebard's work is well remembered.

From the point of view of photography, the immense number of archaeological discoveries made from the air can best be approached by Crawford's classification, which depends on the agricultural state of the ground at the sites. The three conditions which may be differentiated are: land with ancient earthworks intact (a *shadow site*); land which is cultivated but is not growing a crop (a *soil mark* site); and land covered by a crop (a *crop mark* site). The dates and times at which flights must be made, the way in which the early remains appear and the photographic procedures used all depend on which of these three types of sites are under examination.

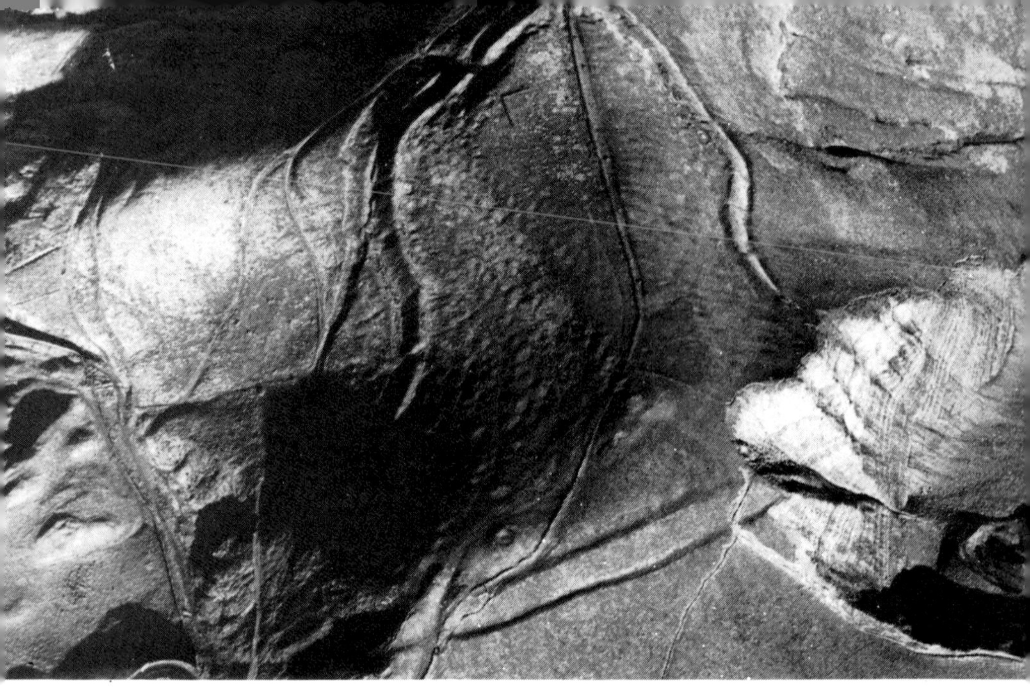

Fig. 1. The hillfort on Mam Tor, Castleton, Derbyshire, on a winter morning. Sunlight emphasises the relief of almost the whole interior surface. (SK 128837. 11.30 a.m. 13th November 1976.)

Fig. 2. The hillfort on Mam Tor on a summer evening. The light of the low sun shows the relief of the western side, but the eastern side is in shadow. (SK 128837. 6.30 p.m. 6th June 1976.)

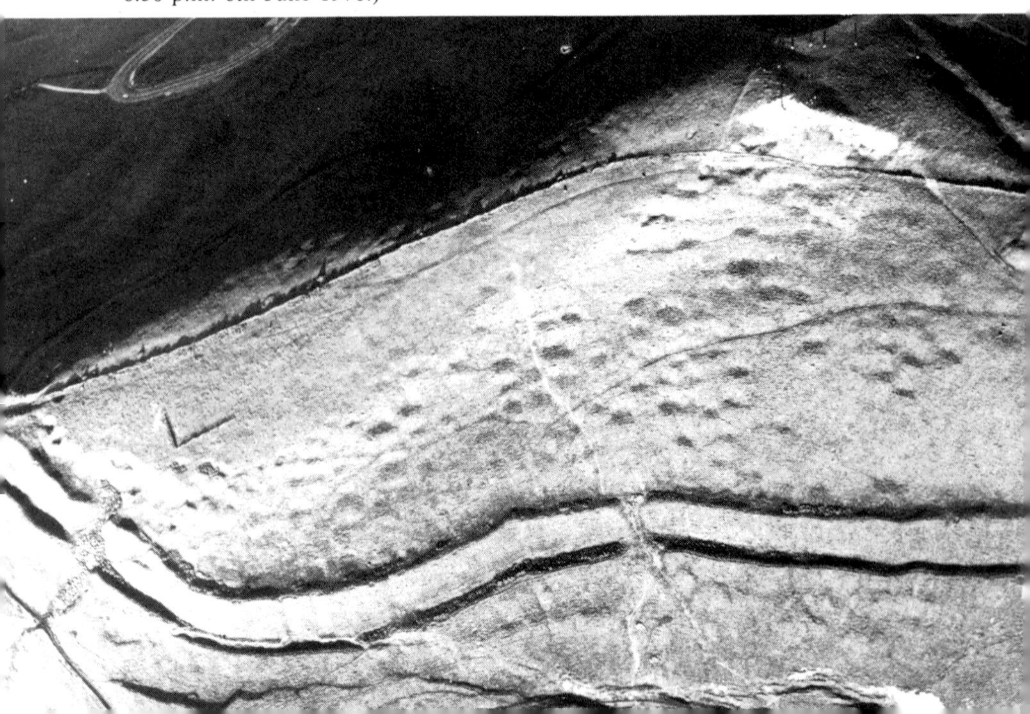

2
Standing earthworks

The value of the aerial view is exemplified by two pictures of the hillfort on Mam Tor, near Castleton, Derbyshire (figs. 1 and 2). The first view (fig. 1), taken in November, is typical of many similar photographs of large earthworks, in which their details are picked out by the shadows thrown when the sun was low in the sky. It is very instructive to see the whole circuit of the defences at one time, though the view minimises the steepness of the cliffs and slopes of Mam Tor, except where they are in shadow. Oblique views of this type may be useful to amplify surveys made on the ground, though when maps are to be made the most useful photographs are verticals, from which it is possible to prepare contoured plans of the site by means of photogrammetry. Mapping methods are described in Chapter 6.

Photographs of large earthworks may also give the details of slight features, inconspicuous on the ground, but of much importance, such as the numerous slight depressions which scar the interior of the Mam Tor fort, in contrast to the smoothness of the surface outside the defences (fig. 1). A second picture of the western side of the fort (fig. 2), taken on a June evening, gives more detail and it can be seen that the depressions are circular house platforms. Excavation has shown that the platforms were cut into the hillside to provide sites for round houses, two of which were dated to the earlier first millennium BC, and although this bleak eminence rises to nearly 1700 feet (520 metres) it was apparently at one time densely inhabited. On fig. 2 the eastern side of the fort is in shadow, and to obtain corresponding detail of the house platforms on that side of the hill during the summer, an early morning flight would have to be made. In the winter months, on the other hand, the sun shining from the south at a low elevation even at midday reveals the detail of almost all the ground surface within the fort (fig. 1). Similarly, when photographing other shadow sites in hilly country, the best dates and times have to be found.

While shadow photography has been an important adjunct to the study of limited areas such as hillforts, its most important application is in the exploration and survey of the low banks, walls and ditches remaining from former systems of fields, abandoned long ago, and the literature about the prehistoric and Roman landscape in Britain is full of references to research from the air.

Britain is still rich in the low earthworks remaining from the work of early farmers, though the rate of destruction of such relics of the past has been deplorable in recent years, because so much old grassland has been taken into plough. Until recently the downs of Sussex, Hampshire, Berkshire, Wiltshire and Dorset had very extensive remains of prehistoric and Roman fields, usually called *Celtic fields*, a name given to them years ago to imply an early date, though the term has little meaning. These fields are small, generally under 0.6 hectares (1½ acres) in area, and are normally rectangular in plan. The picture of Burderop Down, on the Marlborough Downs in Wiltshire (fig. 3), shows Celtic fields on a hillside, where the downhill movement of soil caused by ploughing has formed terraces, called *lynchets*. Shadows outline the scarp at the edge of each lynchet. Across these ancient fields cuts the ditch of a later enclosure.

The picture of Burderop Down was taken with the morning sun in October. The ground at this point slopes to the north and provides good conditions for shadow photography at many times of the year. A different situation is shown by the picture of Green Down, Childrey, Oxfordshire, taken at 8.30 a.m. in November (fig. 4). Celtic fields are here on a slope facing south and the lynchets show by the *highlights* of the picture, where the reflected sunlight is at its brightest, and not by shadow, with the result that the plan shows with less contrast.

Between the fields on Green Down can be seen a lane of the type often described as a *double lynchet way* (marked A to B on fig. 4), its course outlined by the lynchets formed by adjacent fields. The area with numerous shallow depressions and low banks (near B on fig. 4) was no doubt the site of the farm from which the fields were worked, but here the picture is not very informative. There is also a series of large pits of the type dug to extract chalk to spread on the land in relatively recent years. The aerial view gives a wonderful plan of the ancient landscape, but ground survey and excavation of selected spots are essential to elucidate detail fully. No part of the landscape can be given more than a tentative date from an air photograph alone.

The shadow sites of the downs show well because much of the grass was kept short by sheep at the dates when the photographs were taken, and the same may be said about the pastures of Upper Wharfedale in North Yorkshire, shown on figs. 5 and 6, two pictures which show how light falls of snow can be of advantage to the air photographer. Well preserved remains of early field walls are seen

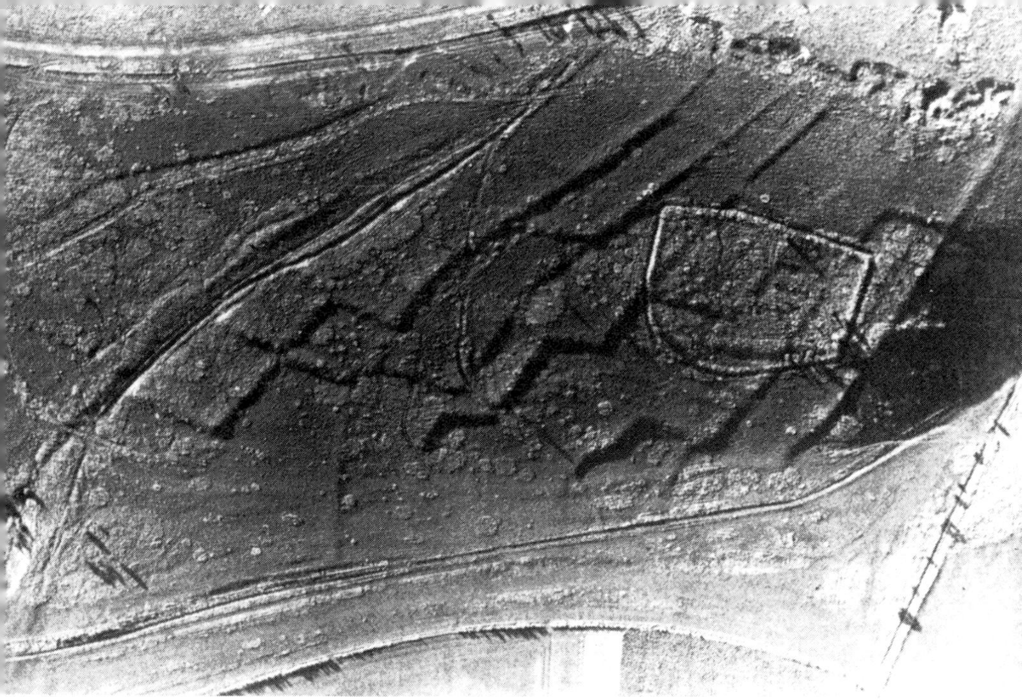

Fig. 3. Celtic fields on Burderop Down, Chiseldon, Wiltshire, shown by shadow on a north-facing slope on an autumn morning. (SU 160765. 8.30 a.m. 22nd October 1943.)

Fig. 4. Celtic fields on Green Down, Childrey, Oxfordshire, shown by highlights on a south-facing slope on a winter morning. From A to B is a 'double lynchet way'. (SU 350840. 8.30 a.m. 25th November 1943.)

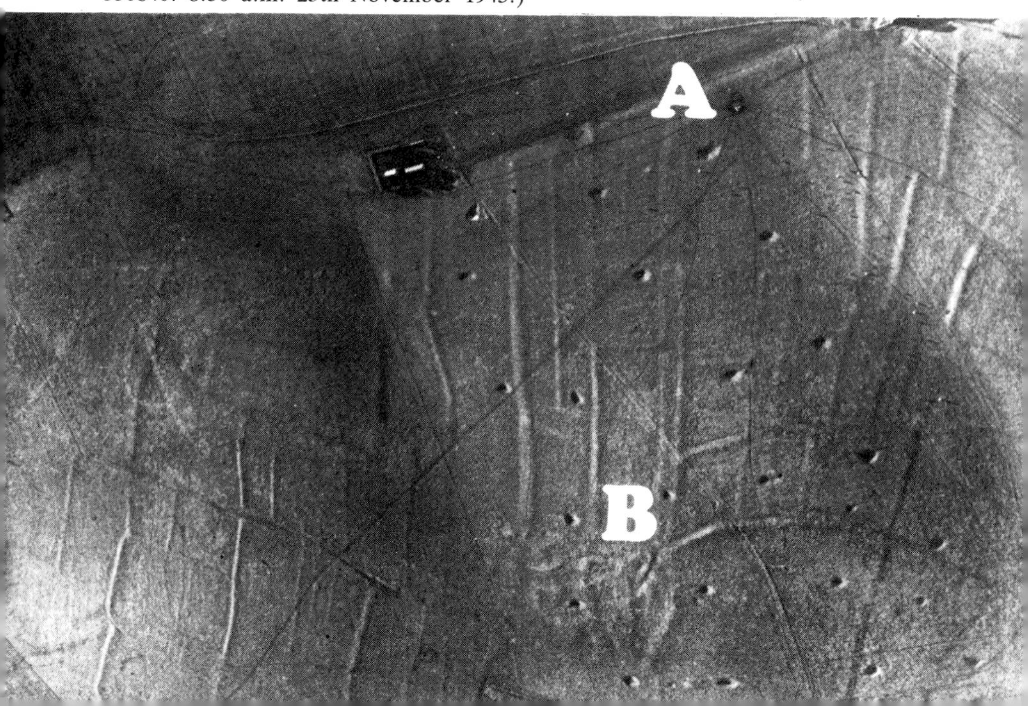

Fig. 5. Remains of ancient field walls (lower right) and of later, perhaps seventeenth-century, ploughing above Hill Castles Scar, Conistone, North Yorkshire, under light snow. (SD 990686. 1 p.m. 27th December 1980.)

Fig. 6. Celtic fields at Grassington, North Yorkshire, under a light covering of snow. (SE 004655. 1 p.m. 27th December 1980.)

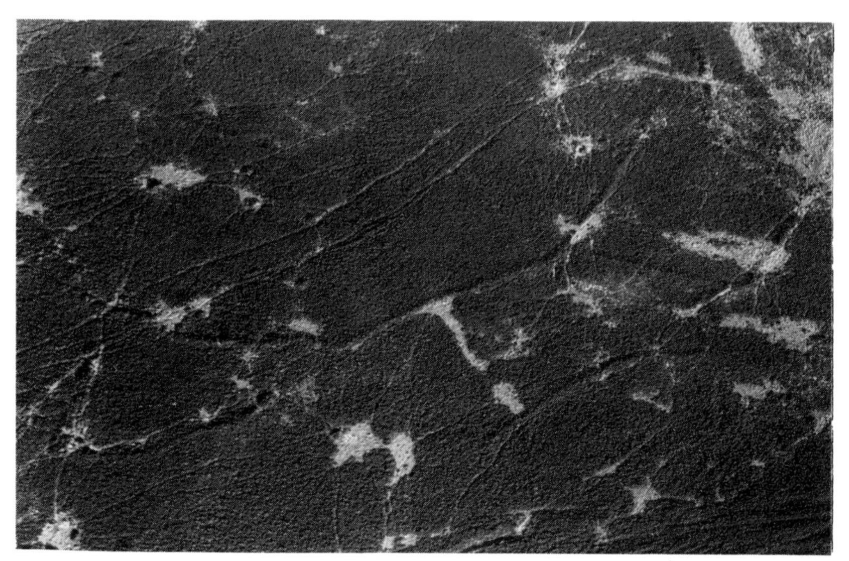

Fig. 7. Early field walls on the heather (dark colour) and grass (light colour) moorland of Big Moor, Baslow, Derbyshire. (SK 272754. 6.30 p.m. 18th May 1976.)

on the lower right-hand corner of fig. 5 and all over fig. 6. The left side and middle distance of fig. 5 also show very distinctly the traces of more recent ploughing, perhaps of seventeenth-century date. When the fig. 5 photograph was taken, a light snowfall covered the whole land surface, except for areas of bare rock, which show as dark patches. Fig. 6 gives a picture taken only a few minutes before fig. 5, but conditions were different, because the land here is at a slightly lesser altitude. The small increase of temperature lower down allowed the snow to melt in places, particularly on low banks which therefore showed as dark lines on the white snow. Where this happened the plan of the ancient fields was outlined in a remarkable way.

On rougher ground shadows are less easy to see because of the camouflaging effect of uneven vegetation, such as the heather growing on the low banks surrounding ancient fields near an earlier bronze age occupation site on Big Moor, Froggatt, Derbyshire (fig. 7). These banks had been surveyed on the ground before they were seen from the air, and aerial pictures with the desired shadows proved difficult to obtain.

Moorland, though its area is shrinking, provides much the largest reserve of country in Britain to have escaped modern ploughing, and on Dartmoor recent exploration has revealed remarkably extensive remains of the early landscape. Fieldwork on the ground, aided by air survey, has traced long lines of low stone walls which are the boundaries of the fields used by farmers in the second millennium BC. The walls, which have the local name of reaves are now in a collapsed state and are preserved under a cover of vegetation. Air survey has been of considerable assistance in the mapping of the Dartmoor reaves by Andrew Fleming and others. They were often traced by differences in vegetation, such as a thin line of gorse, heather or bilberry plants growing above the stony bank and showing against the background of the grass-grown surrounding land.

Among the more interesting earthworks are the Roman military sites, usually either forts for permanent occupation or marching camps for temporary use during a campaign, which are mentioned again in Chapter 5. The majority have been levelled and the land taken into cultivation, but some are still intact, and fig. 8 shows an example of a marching camp which has survived on marginal land high in the Pennines and was discovered from the air by Professor St Joseph. The camp is of the typical playing card outline, though in the picture the shape is distorted by perspective.

Low earthworks remaining from the labours of medieval farmers are still very extensive, though modern agriculture is unfortunately erasing them in numerous places. Much of medieval England was divided into open fields, and their plans can often be traced by the *ridge and furrow* marking the individual strips into which the fields were divided. This corrugation of the surface of the ground resulted from the practice of turning the sod inwards towards the centre as the plough was guided round the narrow plot of land. The strips were usually in blocks, termed furlongs, which often ran at right angles to each other, producing the characteristic patchwork pattern seen on parts of fig. 10. The remains of this system occupy so much land, even now, that they are best recorded as part of a survey made by an aircraft equipped with a vertically mounted camera which takes continuous sets of photographs covering large areas. The survey of the whole of Britain which was made by the RAF after the Second World War is valuable in this respect, because it was made when more ridge and furrow survived than at the present day. There is also much to be gained from other vertical surveys, such as those made for planning authorities by commercial air survey firms, from whom prints can be bought. Such surveys, however, are usually made when the light is good in the middle of the day, rather than at times when there are long shadows to show low earthworks to best advantage.

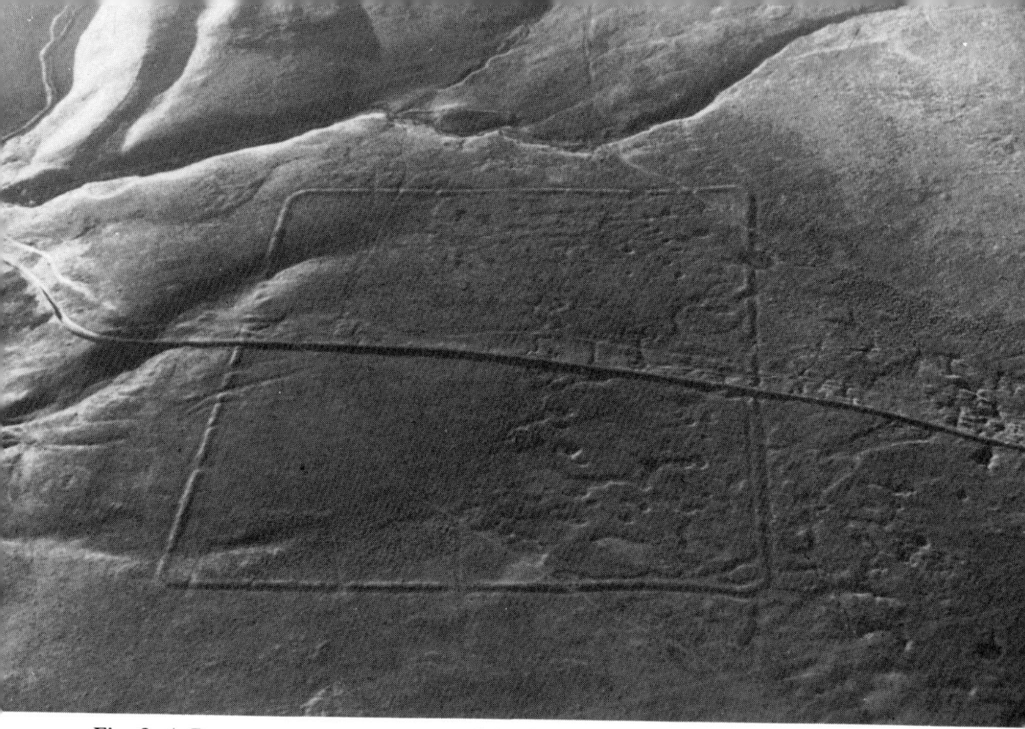

Fig. 8. A Roman temporary camp on Mastiles Moor, Malham, North Yorkshire. (SD 915655. 7.30 p.m. 21st June 1977.)

Fig. 9. Remains of lead mining at Rowter Farm, Castleton, Derbyshire. (SK 127817. 8.30 p.m. 6th June 1976.)

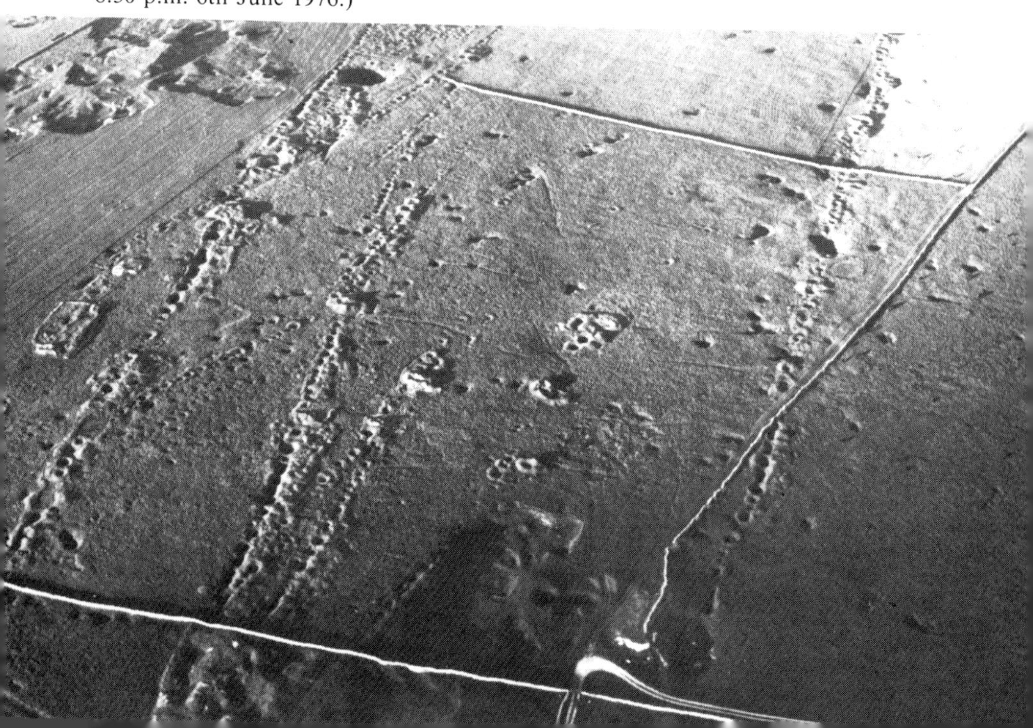

Fig. 10. The shrunken medieval village of Salton, in Ryedale, North Yorkshire. (SE 720800. 2nd April 1980.)

The considerable population of rural England in the middle ages is suggested by the frequent low earthworks which reveal the sites of deserted or shrunken medieval villages: for instance, on fig. 10, near the few houses, farms and the church which comprise Salton in Ryedale, North Yorkshire. The small modern village is surrounded by the remains of its much larger predecessor. The long rectangular plots shown by shadows are the crofts in which were placed the houses of the medieval inhabitants. The ploughland of that time, shown by the ridge and furrow, comes right to the back of the crofts. Excellent photographs of various deserted medieval villages are included in the book *Medieval England; An Aerial Survey* by Professors M. W. Beresford and J. K. S. St Joseph, to which the reader is referred.

The scars left on the surface of the land by mining and quarrying are sometimes so distinct that valuable information may be recorded from the air for industrial archaeologists. In many cases more recent activity has obscured the earlier workings, but this is not always the case. Lead mines, for example, mainly of post-medieval date, look very striking when they follow veins of ore in remote parts of the carboniferous limestone uplands (fig. 9) of the Pennines.

3
Soil marks

Considerable areas of bare soil, the colour of which varies from place to place, are seen from the air in winter and early spring when the ground is being cultivated. Peaty soils are very dark, almost black in places; clay soils are generally darker than the shallow calcareous soils above limestone, and soils above chalk may be very light-coloured. Here and there, where the ploughing has been deeper than usual, light-coloured subsoil may have been brought to the surface. Air photographs of these complicated patterns are used by the Soil Survey in the compilation of soil maps.

Disturbances of the ground generally affect the colour of the surface soil. The course of a modern pipeline, for example, shows clearly because light-coloured material from the subsoil remains on the surface and betrays the position of the trench dug to take the pipe. The archaeologist is interested in the traces of past disturbances of the ground and can learn from soil colours on sites which are under plough, though in most cases soil marks unfortunately represent a stage in the destruction of early remains by the plough (see fig. 12). The mixing of the soil by repeated cultivation causes the marks to become less distinct in successive years, until eventually the surface becomes uniform in composition and they disappear. They may be produced again, however, if deeper ploughing brings to the surface fresh material which had not been reached by earlier ploughing, for example fig. 13.

When earthworks are ploughed for the first time there are considerable differences in the colour of the soil which is turned up on various parts of the site. The soil from the filling of old ditches tends to have a larger content of organic matter and be dark-coloured, and in consequence a dark soil mark generally shows the line of an old ditch. A substantial bank or mound generally incorporates light-coloured subsoil material dug from a deep quarry ditch, and a ploughed bank is therefore normally lighter than the surrounding soil. Figs. 11 and 12 show two enclosures, one larger than the other, on Sutton Common, near Askern, South Yorkshire. The first picture (fig. 11), taken on an evening in July, shows the field when it was a meadow, in which, incidentally, the earthworks were camouflaged by the long uncut grass. The second photograph (fig. 12) was taken after the ploughing of the part of the meadow which

Fig. 11. Two large enclosures or 'camps' on Sutton Common, Norton, South Yorkshire, seen on a summer evening. The shadows are not distinct because of the long grass in the field. (SE 564122. 7.30 p.m. 7th July 1976.)

Fig. 12. The same view as fig. 11 photographed after the larger enclosure had been ploughed. (SE 564122. 29th May 1980.)

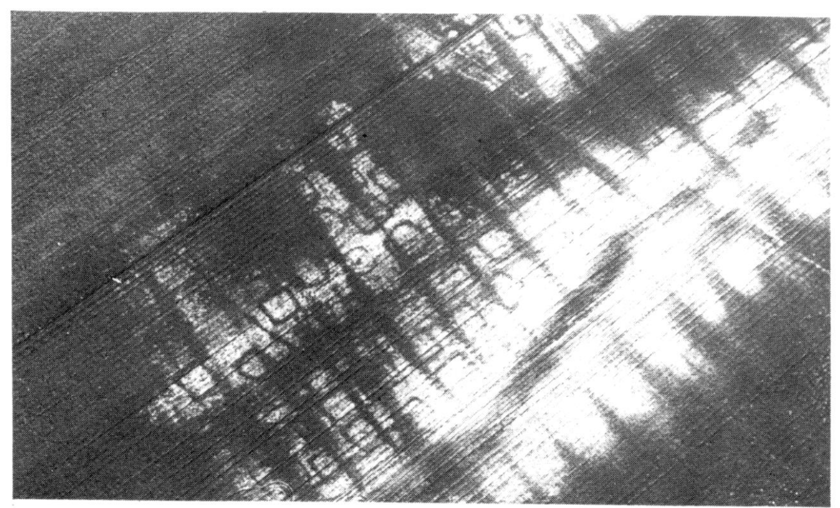

Fig. 13. Soil marks near Springdale Farm, Rudston, North Humberside, show the ditches of iron age square barrows, and in some cases the central graves. The dark bands are the furrows of medieval ridge and furrow ploughing. (TA 092693. 15th February 1981.)

contained the larger of the two enclosures.

Soil marks can convey a great deal of information, but their interpretation is not always straightforward. On fig. 12 the outline of the ploughed enclosure shows well on the left-hand side of the photograph, where two ditches produce dark lines and two very light-coloured strips mark ramparts. A band of pale soil round the whole enclosure marks the inner (and on the right-hand side, the only) rampart, inside which, it is interesting to note, the soil colour is lighter than the very dark soil at the left-hand edge of the picture. The dark soil was the result of marshy conditions, and the area within the ramparts was rather higher and better drained.

When the soil marks on fig. 12 are examined carefully it is seen that they form zigzag lines where the surface has been shifted in alternate directions as the plough has gone up and down the field. This demonstrates the soil movement caused by ploughing, which eventually mixes the surface layers thoroughly.

On the site at Rudston, North Humberside, shown on fig. 13, soil marks had been obliterated by years of ploughing, which had begun in the middle ages, to judge from the dark bands crossing the site, caused by medieval ridge and furrow cultivation. In 1981, however, the marks appeared again after deeper ploughing, which in places had reached the top of the chalk, cutting into the upper layers of the

Fig. 14. Celtic fields under plough at Bull Farm, Kings Worthy, Hampshire. (SU 500350. 14th March 1972.)

Fig. 15. Soil marks (foreground and distance), crop marks (middle distance) and earthworks (upper right-hand side) showing Romano-British fields and a lane at Providence House, Moulton Fen, near Spalding, Lincolnshire. (TF 298140. 8th May 1938.)

ditch fillings of a group of square barrows of iron age date.

The soil marks which have received the most attention are those which are formed on the chalk downs of southern England by the ploughing of the Celtic fields described in Chapter 2. Fig. 14 gives an example photographed at Bull Farm, Kings Worthy, near Winchester. The principal element is a pattern of rectangles marked by light-coloured bands with darker bands on each side. The light-coloured ground shows where the plough has cut into chalk as it passed the scarp of the former lynchet, and the darker-coloured is deeper topsoil. From these soil differences it is possible to reconstruct the plan of the ancient fields which existed as earthworks before modern ploughing commenced on this land.

Another region where air photographs of soil marks have been of primary importance is in the Fens. The silty soil of the northern part of the Fens forms a great tract of land which has much potential if well drained. In Roman times it appears to have been extensively occupied, and large numbers of ditches were cut in connection with farms and settlements in this low lying and wet land. After the Roman period the ditches were abandoned and became filled with peaty material very different in tone from the buff-coloured silty soil of the surrounding land. Ploughing now brings these dark-coloured ditch fillings to the surface, and very distinct and persistent marks are formed. Fig. 15 shows several modern fields where soil marks of this type may be seen, and it also includes two fields with crop marks and one in which the ditches were still earthworks at the date when the photograph was taken.

In addition to the remains of human activity, marks in the soil of the Fenland reveal the positions of former rivers and creeks, which are now traceable by meandering lines or low banks of silt, lighter in tone and often slightly higher than the surrounding land. The local name for these is *roddons* or *rodhams*. In the Fens, therefore, not only do soil marks reveal the remains of the work of the early inhabitants, but also much about the former environment can be learned from them. On occasions both are combined, and there are traces of the diversion of watercourses by man.

During flights made to search for sites of archaeological interest it is advisable to examine any gravel pit, quarry or construction site where the surface soil has been stripped from a large piece of ground as a preliminary operation. Holes dug into the ground in former times may be shown very clearly at such sites by their darker-coloured fillings. The value of the distant view is well demonstrated by fig. 16, which shows a site at Rothwell, near Leeds, photographed when the surface soil was being removed in preparation for use of

Fig. 16. A rectangular ditched enclosure at Rothwell, West Yorkshire, on land from which the topsoil has been removed by earth-moving machines. (SE 354295. 1st August 1977.)

the land as a colliery tip. A faint dark rectangle with rounded corners can be seen in the middle of the picture on the area of light ground, which is an exposed patch of coal measures sandstone. The site was visited on foot very soon after it had been discovered from the air, but the rectangle was located only with great difficulty because the ground had been so much churned up by the heavy earth-moving machinery. The dark line is the lowest part of the filling of a ditch, from which unfortunately no certain evidence of date was obtained when the site was excavated, though inside the rectangle was a deep rock-cut well containing much material of Roman date.

Soil colours do not stay exactly the same during the winter, and both weathering of the soil and changes of its water content have distinct effects. The most interesting result of differences in soil moisture is the *taches d'humidité* (damp marks) seen frequently in northern France by R. Agache. They are caused by a different rate of drying of the ground above buried features, the plans of which are thus shown by lines of damper, and hence darker soil. These marks occur when the land is drying after a wet spell, and they often disappear in a matter of hours. Although similar damp marks are seldom reported in Britain, they may well prove to be important on some soils.

4
Crop marks and their causes

It has long been known that buried remains could be traced by their effect on crops growing above them, that is by *crop marks*. Various early antiquaries reported such phenomena, though few were as careful as Stephen Stone, an Oxford don, who in 1857 recorded thirteen rings in the corn at Standlake, Oxfordshire. He subsequently excavated the site and fig. 17 is the plan given in the report on the site published in *Archaeologia*, volume 37.

Because so much of Britain, except for the moors and mountains, is cultivated farmland, crop marks are much the most important source of information to be recorded by the air photographer. They only occur when conditions are right, however, and before describing some of the results obtained by aerial exploration, it will be helpful to summarise the rather complex factors which determine where and when they are likely to occur. A convenient point at which to start is a photograph taken by G. W. G. Allen (fig. 18) of a crop mark (shown by an arrow) sectioned by the face of a gravel pit near Oxford. The pit had cut into a field of standing corn with a crop mark composed of darker-coloured and taller plants. The picture shows the crop and the soil on which it was growing, and below, cut into the gravel, can be seen the filling of an old ditch, directly under the crop mark. With this photograph as a basis, a diagram (fig. 19 A and B) may be drawn to illustrate the enhancement of crop growth on deeper soil to produce what may be called a *positive crop mark* (figs. 20 to 32), and the reduced growth which may be termed a *negative crop mark*, caused when the soil depth is reduced by a buried Roman road (fig. 34), buried wall foundations (fig. 33) or some other obstruction to root penetration. The great majority of crop marks are of the positive variety, and they are most often seen in cereals – barley, wheat and oats – though they occur also in other crops, of which more will be said later.

The most important cause of the marks appears to be the effects of drought when the crop is growing. It is noticeable that there are many distinct marks to be seen in cereal crops when the early summer months are dry, and conversely that only a few faint marks appear when this period is wet. During the summer, rainfall is normally insufficient to replace losses of water from the soil by evaporation, which are greatly increased by the large amounts of moisture extracted from the ground and transpired through the

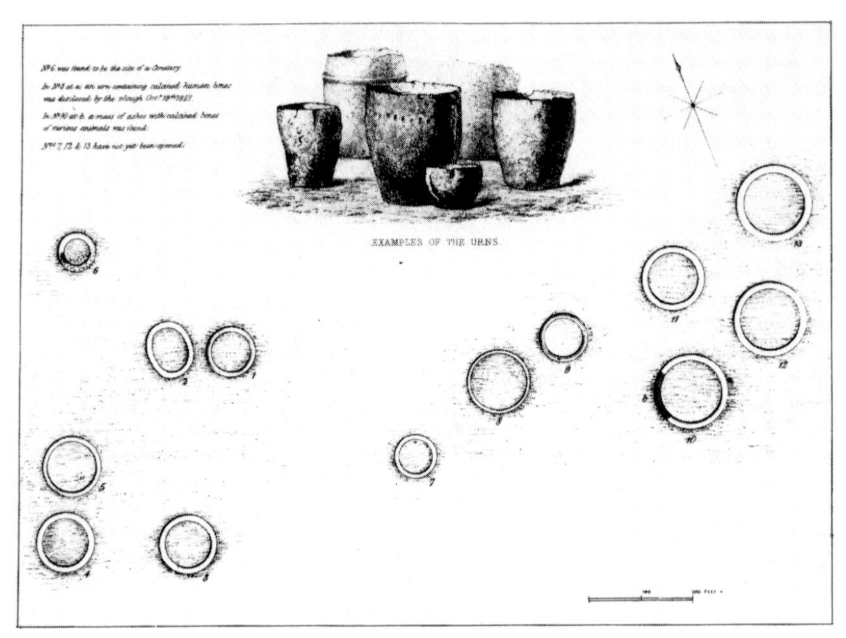

Fig. 17. A group of ring ditches at Standlake, Oxfordshire, planned in 1857 by Stephen Stone from marks in a cornfield. (SP 385045.)

Fig. 18. Section of a crop mark (shown by an arrow) at the former Allen's gravel pit at Dorchester, Oxfordshire. At this point the pit cut into the filling of the ditch of an iron age enclosure, above which was a crop of standing corn. (SU 575965. 7th July 1938.)

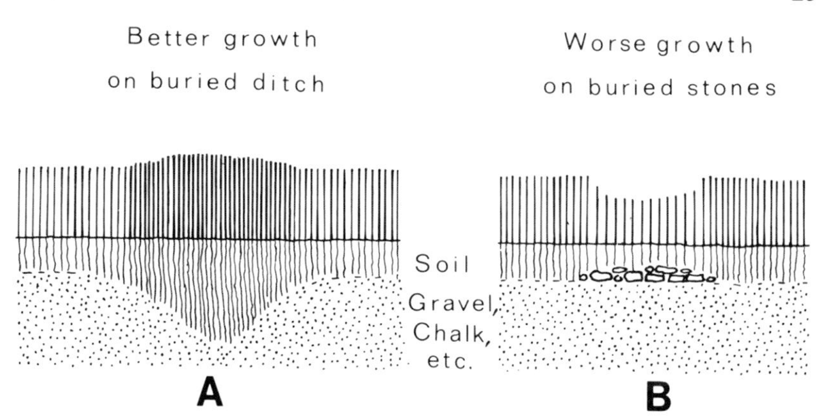

Fig. 19. Diagram of (A) positive crop mark, (B) negative crop mark.

leaves of vegetation. This moisture deficit is made up by water stored in the soil during winter, but a point may come at which this is exhausted and the soil becomes very dry. Crops then may begin to flag, or suffer from *moisture stress*, except on the patches of deeper soil, such as the fillings of old ditches and pits where the deeper rooting zone holds more reserves of moisture.

Crop marks may also result from differences of germination after the seeds have been sown. In a very dry spring it is sometimes noticed that the plants are much more forward above the fillings of old ditches, where the deeper soil has held the necessary moisture for germination to proceed when the surrounding soil has become too dry (for example fig. 20). Where there are pronounced soil differences in a field, early germination may also be caused by factors such as the peaty filling of old ditches in the silty soil of the northern Fens, where the crop marks may be seen in spring even in wet weather.

The dates for sowing of cereals may be important. It is possible for two adjacent fields, one with winter sown and the other with spring sown corn, to behave quite differently. If, for example, there were a wet period in May and June, followed by a drought in July, the winter sown field might ripen in July without having been subjected to moisture shortage in the growing period when the plants were green, in which case there would be no crop marks in the field that season. Alternatively, in the spring sown field the July drought might catch the crop while it was still green, and distinct crop marks might develop in consequence.

Fig. 20. Crop marks at Lodge Farm, North Muskham, Nottinghamshire, probably caused by differences of germination in the dry spring of 1976. Enclosures, lanes and two pit alignments were shown by shine and by relief when looking towards the sun; looking with the sun they could hardly be seen.(SK 798600. 6th June 1976.)

The positive marks seen in cereal crops are usually darker green than the rest of the field around them while the crop is growing (for example fig. 21), and when it is ripening and turning yellow they often, but by no means always, remain for a limited period as green lines in a yellow field, showing up with great contrast, as in the cover photograph. Frequently there are also lines of taller and denser growth, which may show by shadow (fig. 20). Such lines of dense growth are probably the reason why the marks often continue to show as *lighter*-coloured lines, sometimes called *crop reversal marks* (fig. 22), after the crop has ripened and the plants have everywhere become light yellow in colour. A further possibility is for the plants forming the crop mark to collapse, or become *lodged* or *laid* in bad weather, in which case the mark appears in yet another guise (fig. 23).

None of the other crops have the same complications for the aerial archaeologist. Sugar beet can show buried features very well (figs. 27 and 31), and marks in it begin to form in late July, when the corn harvest has started; alternatively the vagaries of the weather may prevent their appearance until well into August, if at all. Other root

Fig. 21. Ring ditches at Foxley Farm, Eynsham, Oxfordshire, early in the summer. (SP 425084. 5th June 1933.)

Fig. 22. The same view as fig. 21 photographed after the corn had ripened. (SP 425084. 16th July 1933.)

crops may also have marks useful to the archaeologist, except potatoes, which show little. Peas, beans, clover and lucerne may be good for our purpose, though the dates of appearance of the marks may be spread over some weeks.

Grass is a special case. Darker green positive marks seldom have as much contrast as in cereals, though there are very clear marks in a grass field on the left side of fig. 21. Negative marks can, however, show well in this crop — a word correctly used to describe grass on farms, though a misnomer on parks and sports grounds, which should not be forgotten when making air surveys. These marks may develop distinctly as a result of parching of the grass above former building foundations and are often called parch marks, but the use of a special term for grass is a source of confusion and there is no reason why marks in grass should be described differently from marks in any other crop.

The dates of appearance of crop marks and their duration can vary considerably. The weather, the soil, the various crops and their dates of sowing interact to produce marks at different dates during the late spring and summer. When a thorough survey of a district is to be made there seems to be no alternative to flights about once a fortnight from April to August, and at least every week if and when cereals begin to show marks well, probably in June. The dates of the flying campaign can be postponed for perhaps a month in the north of England and Scotland, where the growing season is later. Air photographers watch cereals – barley, wheat and oats – with special care during dry spells in June or July because, despite factors which cause one field to behave differently from another, marks in these crops can then be visible at the same time at many places.

In addition to the crops and the weather, it is necessary to know something of the soils and the underlying rocks of the district which is being surveyed, since they also have a great influence on the formation of crop marks. The means by which this occurs may vary, but the most important appears to be that soils above deposits such as gravels or sands give up moisture steadily in times of drought until no more is available, after which there is a cut-off point. In these circumstances the plants on thinner soil exhaust the available moisture and begin to suffer moisture stress, while other plants continue to flourish on the deeper soil of the filling of an old ditch. A positive crop mark therefore appears along the line of the ditch filling. Gravel is usually very conducive to the formation of crop marks, and they may also become distinct above sand, chalk and limestone, though the variable hardness of the last named rock has effects which are sometimes unforeseen. Soft and rubbly limestone

Fig. 23. Crop marks of early land boundaries at Hotham, North Humberside, showing lines of collapsed ('lodged') corn in the central field. (SE 878343. 7th July 1976.)

below the surface soil may have had many cuttings made into it by early man, and there may then be many crop marks, while if the rock near the surface is hard the reverse generally applies. Further variations are caused by the depth of the surface soil; where its depth exceeds about 500 millimetres (20 inches) the effects of ditch fillings become less pronounced, and soil 1 metre (40 inches) deep does not normally produce the marks.

Clay is usually unfavourable to crop mark formation, though there are exceptions. In dry weather clay soils give up moisture differently; they release it at a progressively reduced rate but do not have a cut-off point like sandy or gravelly soils, so pronounced differences of crop growth are much less likely to appear. Low lying clay soils, such as those in parts of the Lincolnshire and Cambridgeshire Fens, may, however, have well defined crop marks above the humose filling of old ditches.

The great differences in the capacity of the soil to produce crop marks in different areas must be remembered when examining distribution maps of ancient sites in which the results of air survey have been incorporated. Large numbers of sites may have been marked on land with, say, a gravel subsoil, and only a few on land which is based on clay. There may well have been many sites in the latter areas, but because clays are normally unfavourable to crop mark formation these sites will not have been seen from the air and put on the map.

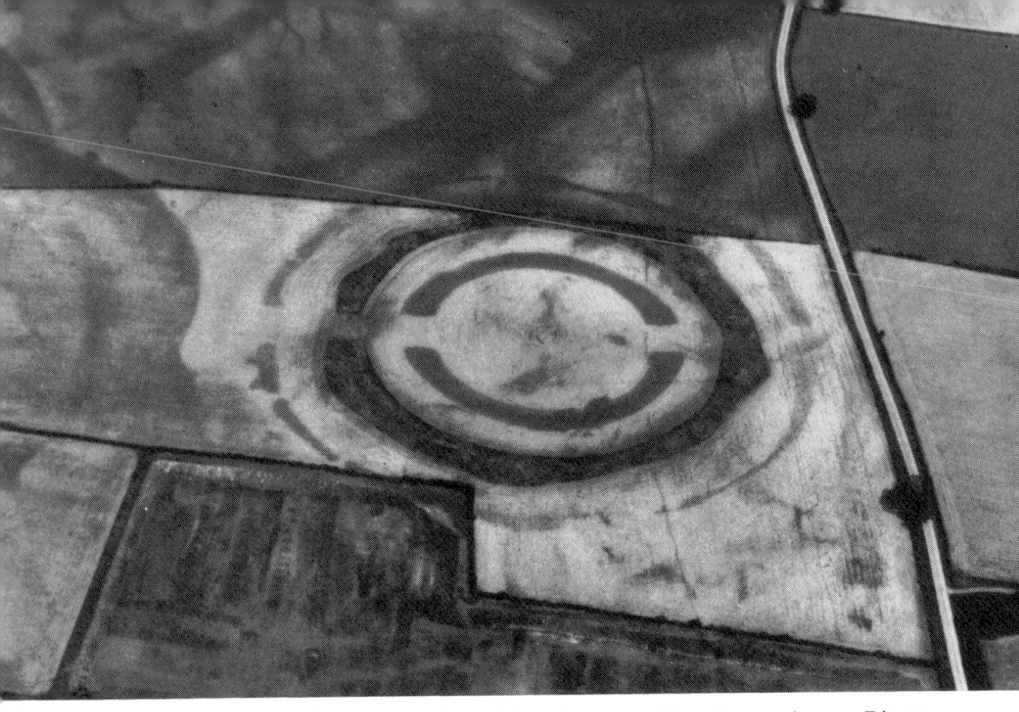

Fig. 24. The central henge in the line of three henges at Thornborough, near Ripon, North Yorkshire. The bank is still an earthwork but the inner and outer ditches are crop marks. The two parallel ditches of the cursus intersect the henge. (SE 285794. 10th July 1976.)

Fig. 25. The cursus and several ring ditches at Drayton, near Abingdon, Oxfordshire. (SU 485936. 12th July 1933.)

5
The interpretation of crop marks

Air photographs show something which has been seen briefly and from a distance. The picture must be interpreted to obtain the information which is recorded by various shades of colour, or, in the case of black and white photographs, various shades of grey. Interpretation is always uncertain when it comes to making decisions about the finer details, though when dealing with shadow pictures the site can be visited on the ground to resolve problems, and soil marks may sometimes be elucidated by reference to records of previously existing earthworks. Crop marks are often more difficult, because they show the buried remains indirectly, through the medium of crops, which also have marks caused naturally or by modern agriculture. Further, they only show the part of the ancient remains which is left below the surface after the upper part has been levelled by the plough.

Only the most approximate date can normally be given to a site seen from the air. A limited amount of information may come from field walking, from excavation of adjacent sites and, in the case of medieval remains, from documents. In most cases, however, the only information given by air photographs about a crop mark is its plan. These plans must therefore be analysed, any associations with other crop marks or standing earthworks noted, and comparison made with excavated sites. Interesting points may emerge, for instance at the site at Rossington, South Yorkshire, mapped on fig. 42, a Roman road cuts across some ancient fields, which were presumably in use before the road was made.

The following accounts describe very briefly the principal types of remains which may produce crop marks in Britain. Since size and shape are the main criteria, there is something to be said for listing the types under the headings of geometrical shape, but this would place them in a somewhat confusing order – for example rectangles could include a neolithic cursus, iron age square barrows, Roman forts and camps, and enclosures of many dates. It has therefore been thought better to list the types of sites in approximate date order. It must be remembered, however, that when a rectangle is seen the interpreter has to make a choice between widely different possibilities.

EARLY RITUAL SITES: LARGER SIZE

(a) Henges

The late neolithic or bronze age monuments called henges consist of large circular banks with one or two entrances, an internal ditch, and sometimes also an external ditch. The illustration (fig. 24) shows the henge at Thornborough, near Ripon, North Yorkshire, which still has its bank and was known long before the days of air photography. The crop marks show well the shapes of the inner ditch and the curiously irregular outer ditch.

(b) Causewayed enclosures

Although the causewayed enclosures (formerly called causewayed camps) of neolithic date have been familiar in southern England since the 1920s, it was not until recent years that further examples were found from the air. There are now above thirty known, of which about half have been recognised from crop marks. The new discoveries have extended the distribution to the Midlands. Reproductions of some of the photographs are given in the paper mentioned in the reading list.

(c) Cursuses

The very long parallel-sided enclosures of neolithic date, called cursuses, are among the most surprising features of the prehistoric landscape. Two have long been known near Stonehenge, but many other examples have been found from the air. Fig. 25 shows the end of the cursus at Drayton, Oxfordshire, and fig. 24 part of the cursus which intersects a henge at Thornborough. At the latter place excavation confirmed that the cursus was the older of the two monuments, a fact which the photograph suggests.

EARLY RITUAL SITES: SMALLER SIZE

(a) Ring ditches

In some parts of England the most noticeable crop marks are rings from 10 to 30 metres (30 to 100 feet) in diameter. They may occur singly, in small numbers, or in quite large groups, such as that at Foxley Farm, Eynsham, Oxfordshire (figs. 21 and 22). In most cases the ring is caused by a single ditch, but sometimes two or even three concentric rings are seen. The shape may depart from the circular, for example the oval on figs. 21 and 22 and the curious shape on the cover picture, which appears to be formed from two rings partly dug and then joined together.

Many ring ditches have now been excavated and they have often

Fig. 26. A large group of square barrows at the bottom of a 'slack' or dry valley at Grindale, near Bridlington, North Humberside. Note also the envelope pattern in the field. (TA 149720. 28th July 1975.)

Fig. 27. An oval enclosure, inside which is a 'fan' shape, and outside field boundary ditches running in various directions, seen in a sugar beet crop at Bilby Farm, near Worksop, Nottinghamshire. (SK 640824. 20th July 1977.)

been found to contain graves of bronze age date. The positions of grave pits are sometimes indicated by small crop marks. In some places, such as the example shown from Thixendale, North Yorkshire (fig. 37), the rings surround ploughed-out round barrows, the remains of which cause a central patch of dark crop marking. Many of the ring ditches may have originally surrounded barrows which have been completely levelled by ploughing, but there are various cases where excavation did not support such a hypothesis, and some rings shown by crop marks were apparently caused by a ditch and bank with no central mound.

Ring ditches of the kind just described may be difficult to distinguish from the circular trenches dug when iron age round houses were constructed. Factors suggesting a house are proximity to an occupation site, and a wide entrance on one side of the ring. The ring inside a rectangle on fig. 28 is probably a house site.

(b) Square barrows

In eastern Yorkshire there are large numbers of crop marks caused by the ditches of the iron age square barrows already mentioned in the chapter on soil marks. They occur not only singly and in groups, like the ring ditches described above, but also in closely packed cemeteries, such as that at Grindale, near Bridlington, which is shown on fig. 26.

RURAL SETTLEMENTS SHOWN BY ENCLOSURES

The most frequent causes of crop marks are the ditched enclosures which in most cases probably marked the positions of occupation sites of different kinds. The crop marks of the enclosures may be accompanied by numerous spots indicating groups of pits, and by circles on round house sites, but these are the exception rather than the rule. The enclosures may occur singly or in groups, some of which may be very complex.

Enclosures vary in area from as little as 200 square metres (2,000 square feet) to as much as 1 hectare (2½ acres), and many different shapes are seen, though the frequency of curvilinear forms and rectangular and sub-rectangular forms suggests traditional forms of planning. Several examples are given: an isolated rounded enclosure (fig. 27), an isolated rectangular enclosure (fig. 28), and a group of enclosures (fig. 29). On figs. 28 and 29 there appear to be traces of a house within the enclosure. These examples do not show signs of recutting of the ditches, but this is often evident, and the overlapping of enclosures is also a sign that these sites often had a long and complicated history of use.

Fig. 28. A rectangular enclosure containing a probable round house site at Bursea Grange, Holme on Spalding Moor, North Humberside. Note also the crop marks caused by modern land drainage. (SE 817343. 4th July 1976.)

Fig. 29. A complex of enclosures and connected field boundaries at Forest Farm, Babworth, Nottinghamshire. (SK 660798. 7th July 1975.)

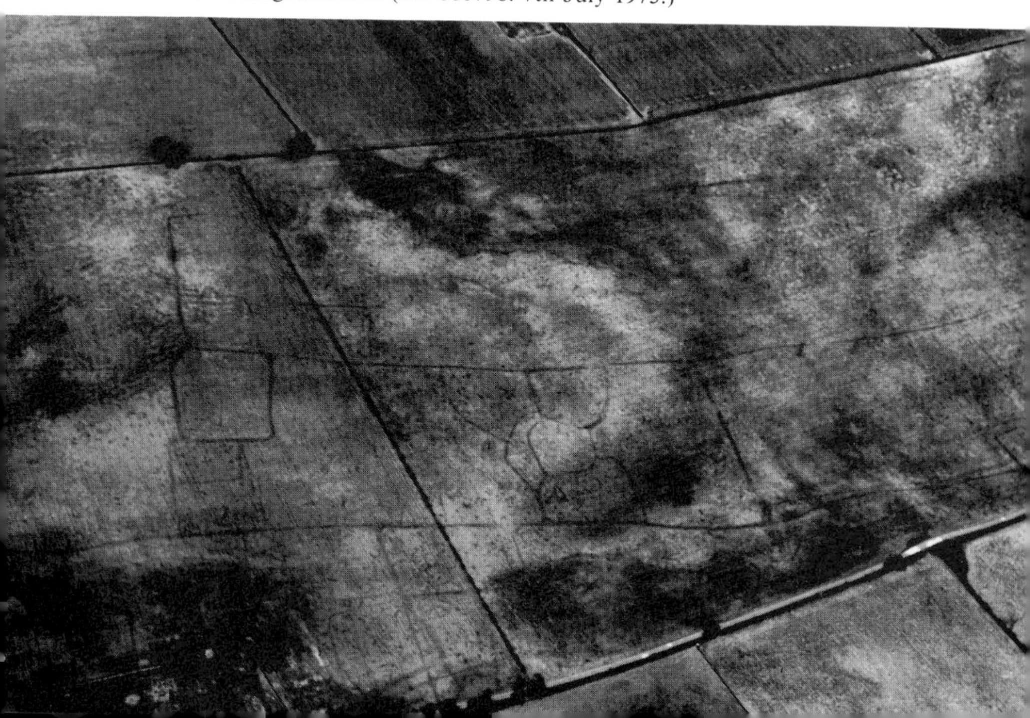

To judge from those which have been excavated, the use of enclosures became common in the bronze age, but most examples were in use in the iron age and Roman periods, when population was greater. The ground within excavated enclosures is often found to contain a mass of features such as post holes, which are too small to form crop marks. When examining air photographs, it is therefore advisable to remember that the crop marks may be only the tip of the iceberg and that there is probably much more below the surface which cannot be seen.

FORTIFICATIONS

The defences of many British hillforts are so big that they have usually survived as earthworks, but this is not always the case, and some have been completely levelled by agriculture and only rediscovered as crop marks. Smaller fortifications are more likely to have been ploughed down, for example, the interesting small circular fort at Thwing, North Humberside (fig. 30), which was shown by the marks of two concentric ditches. Excavations have revealed within the outer ditch the remains of a strong rampart of later bronze age date. Inside this rampart was the inner ditch, which is still not fully explained and may be considerably earlier in date. When first found, this site was interpreted as a henge with two ditches, but excavation is producing a more complicated explanation – an example of the problems of interpreting crop marks from the photographs alone.

FIELDS AND RURAL BOUNDARIES

(a) Fields

In some places extensive networks of boundary ditches define the plans of former fields. The regularly planned fields of the Bunter Sandstone belt of Nottinghamshire and South Yorkshire are seen on figs. 31, 32 and 42, and other field boundaries on low lying land in the Vale of York are seen on fig. 23. Early fields are also very clearly shown by marks of ditches on large areas of the Silt Fens in Lincolnshire and Cambridgeshire (fig. 15). In these regions, and certain others, the field plans can be linked with the crop marks of enclosures which were probably the sites of early farmsteads, and the former landscape can be reconstructed over large tracts of country. This is one of the most important applications of air photography.

(b) Boundary dykes

From the bronze age onwards many major early land boundaries

Fig. 30. A small circular hillfort of bronze age date and double ditched boundary dykes at Paddock Hill, Thwing, North Humberside. (TA 030707. 8th August 1979.)

Fig. 31. Field boundaries seen in a sugar beet crop on Green Mile Farm, Babworth, near Retford, Nottinghamshire. (SK 661812. 5th August 1977.)

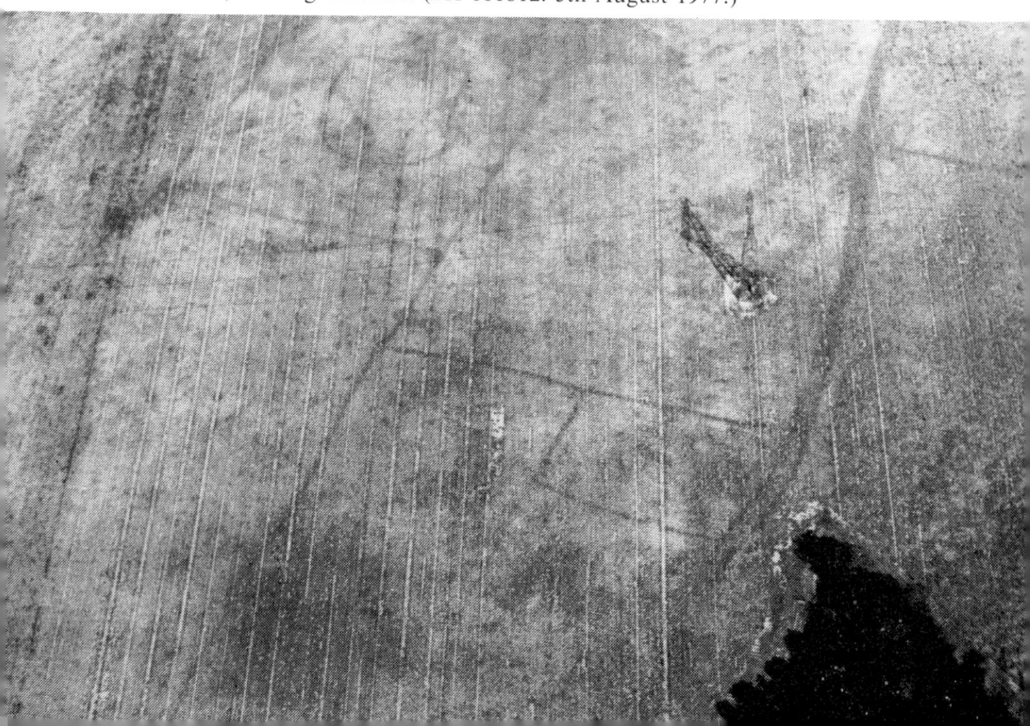

were marked by one or more large ditches and banks, for example on the chalklands of Wessex and the Yorkshire Wolds, and in the Midlands, where Jim Pickering has recently found many previously unknown dykes, which were evidently of some importance. The crop marks seen in the foreground of fig. 30 indicate the course of two ditches of a dyke which ran for over 12 kilometres (7½ miles) on the Yorkshire Wolds. It may be noted that the sharp double bend in the right-hand lower corner of the picture was probably the result of different alignments of their work by two gangs of labourers.

(c) Pit alignments

The boundaries formed by lines of pits, which are revealed by crop marks in many parts of Britain, were almost unknown before the advent of aerial examination of the countryside. They typically consist of long lines of pits perhaps a metre (40 inches) in depth and in diameter, and the same distance apart. Two examples seen on fig. 20 were apparently connected with a cluster of enclosures. Pit alignments are commonly seen in some parts of England, notably the Midlands, and they normally appear to have been land boundaries of a less important type than those shown on fig. 30. There is not much dating evidence, but the little which has been obtained suggests that their use began in the later bronze age and continued in the iron age.

ROMAN BUILDINGS, ROADS AND MILITARY STATIONS

This section describes the more formal kinds of remains of Roman times, but in spite of their number and importance it must be remembered that the most frequent traces of Romano-British activity seen from the air are the extraordinarily numerous enclosures and settlement sites mentioned previously.

(a) Villas and towns

Where the footings of walls have survived the destructive effects of modern ploughing they should produce negative crop marks. An excellent example is given by fig. 33, which shows part of the Roman town of Silchester with the plans of various buildings, including a circular temple (actually the temple, excavated in the nineteenth century, was sixteen-sided), and a small part of the road network. A distant view (fig. 34) gives the road plan of the whole town, within its circuit of walls.

The importance of aerial archaeology in the reconstruction of the early landscape has already been mentioned, and if conditions are right this approach may be of special value near Romano-British

Fig. 32. Field boundaries at Rossington, South Yorkshire. (SK 635987. 27th June 1976.)

Fig. 33. Negative crop marks at Silchester, Hampshire, show roads and buildings, including an apparently round (actually sixteen-sided) temple. (SU 642627. 16th June 1975.)

towns and villas. The latter were the centres of important estates, but little is known about most of the numerous excavated sites except the details of the buildings.

(b) Roads

Air photography has often been used to illustrate the straight line of Roman roads by means of spectacular distant views. Crop marks can be useful in providing more detailed information on the lines of roads, though this happens less often than may be hoped for by archaeologists. As at Silchester, the line of roads may be revealed by negative crop marks where the gravel of a former metalled surface remains below the ploughsoil. Conversely, positive marks may show the line of the ditches which ran a short distance to each side of the road. On the example given on fig. 35, rather faint but unmistakable marks show the side ditches both of the road which runs south-east from York and of a minor road which branches off at B on the photograph.

(c) Roman military stations

Comparison of the Ordnance Survey map of Roman Britain published in 1978 with a much earlier edition of the same map issued in 1928 shows a tremendous advance of knowledge, including a very large number of new military stations, most of which are in Wales, the Welsh Marches, the north of England and Scotland. Much the most important source of new discoveries of military stations has been air reconnaissance, and their substantial defences may produce crop marks even in places where conditions are not too favourable. They are usually recognisable by their playing card shape (for example figs. 8 and 43).

The more important types of Roman military stations to have been located from the air in any number are as follows.

description	*typical size*	*purpose*
vexillation fortress	10 ha	occupation by a detachment (Latin, *vexillatio*) of a legion.
fort	1 to 2 ha	permanent use by an auxiliary unit
marching camp	2 to 20 ha	temporary stopping place by a campaigning force or army

The larger of these establishments seldom fall within the bounds of a single modern field, so that normally only part of the defences can be seen at any one time. The photograph of the vexillation

Fig. 34. Distant view of Silchester. X marks the site of the temple shown on fig. 33. (SU 642627. 3rd August 1972.)

Fig. 35. The line of a Roman road (A to B) and a branch road (starts at B) at Wilberfoss, North Humberside. Early field boundaries are also visible. (SE 745512). 4th July 1976.)

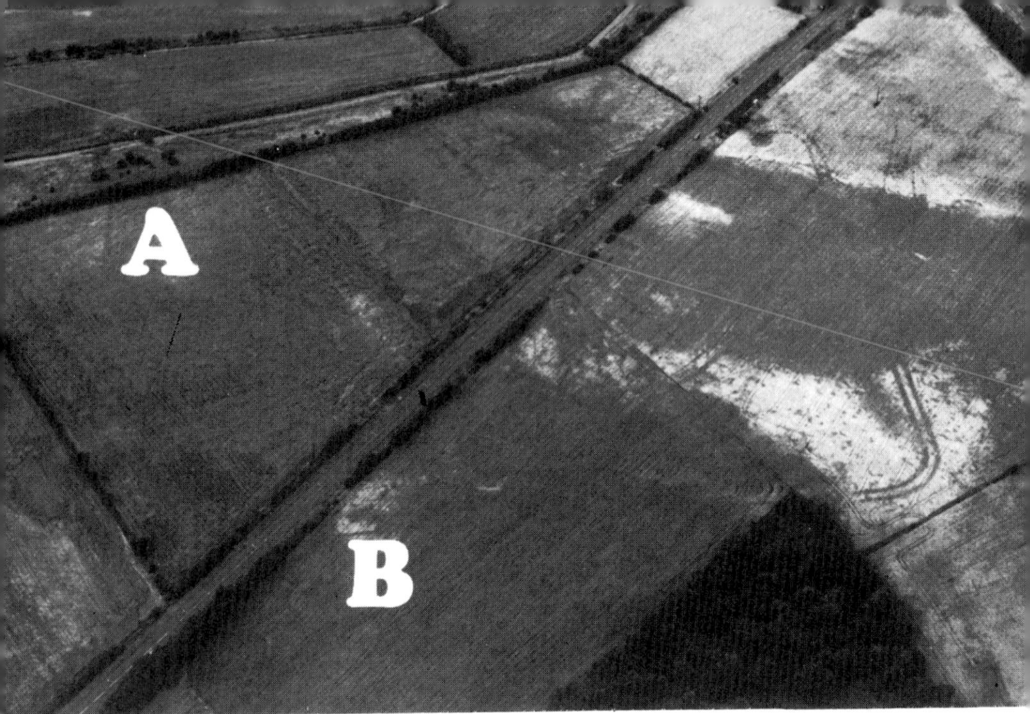

Fig. 36. The Roman vexillation fortress at Rossington, South Yorkshire. The corners of the double-ditch eastern side show well and short lengths of two other sides can be seen at A and B. (SK 628990. 23rd July 1977.) See also fig. 42.

Fig. 37. Indistinct marks of two round barrows and prominent marks caused by current farm work, including the envelope pattern, on Thixendale Wold, North Yorkshire. (SE 855583. 8th August 1979.)

fortress at Rossington, South Yorkshire (fig. 36), shows the defensive ditch at four phases where the soil conditions were suitable for crop mark formation. The ditch was double on the eastern side (right-hand side of picture).

The smaller marching camps are usually of the playing card shape, but the largest, which may be up to 50 or even 60 hectares (120 to 150 acres) in size, may be of irregular outline necessitated by the need to accommodate the defences to the lie of the land. Marching camps may have their entrances defended by a short traverse often referred to as a *titulum*, or by a curved bank termed a *clavicula* (a Latin word meaning key, used because the shape resembles a kind of Roman key). A straight length of ditch with a gap defended by a titulum may be an important clue, and continued observation of the site in subsequent years may produce the rest of the plan of a marching camp.

THE LANDSCAPE

Archaeological remains are customarily described as 'sites', a word which implies a specific location. It will have become apparent to the reader, however, that the early remains visible from the air are exceedingly numerous and are spread over large areas of ground in regions where conditions are suitable for their appearance. In these circumstances the use of the word 'site' often becomes inappropriate, because what is seen is part of a whole 'landscape'. The map reproduced on fig. 42 shows a small part of the extensive landscape recorded in South Yorkshire and north Nottinghamshire by the author through the medium of crop marks. This map shows a Roman road, a Roman fort and many ancient fields. The dates of these remains are at present a matter of speculation, and excavation will be necessary to provide further information, but it is the study of a small collection of air photographs (including figs. 32 and 36) which has provided all the data recorded on this map, and there is no other means by which the matter could have been taken so far without great expense.

MARKS CAUSED BY MODERN AGRICULTURE OR OF GEOLOGICAL ORIGIN

In addition to marks of archaeological interest, air photographs of crops show marks due to many other causes. Some of these may be the result of current farm work or of recent civil engineering activity and others may be due to natural causes, but all have to be understood and correctly interpreted, so that they can be separated

Fig. 38. Crop marks caused by fissures in the underlying limestone rock, and at X an enclosure, at Brodsworth, South Yorkshire. (SE 530050. 29th July 1979.)

Fig. 39. Crop marks caused by frost cracking of the underlying gravel at Redbridge, Greater London. The cracks originated at a time of periglacial climatic conditions. (TQ 460984. 30th June 1977.)

from the archaeological crop marks which may be mixed with them. The most important are probably those caused by the current year's work on the farm and those of geological origin.

Lines caused by drilling the seed, the application of fertiliser or the wheels of a tractor which has gone up and down in a field spraying the crop with weedkiller are very easy to recognise because they are systematic and parallel to modern field boundaries (figs. 37 and 39). Once one knows what it is, the *envelope pattern* (figs. 26 and 37) also causes no difficulty; it is the result of the turning points of farm machinery opposite the corners of fields. The regular pattern, often of herringbone type, caused by land drains often shows clearly (fig. 28); rotating irrigation sprays can make large circles, and many other marks may result from other agricultural causes too numerous to mention.

Limestone can often be recognised from the air by the network of crop marks which form on fissures in the rock underlying the surface soil (fig. 38). These lines may be very regular and may be difficult to distinguish from crop marks caused by human activities. A somewhat similar, though irregular, polygonal pattern (fig. 39 and cover picture) arises from the effects of periglacial conditions in the ice age, when cracks formed in the frozen ground, as they do in arctic regions at the present day. When active, these fissures were filled with ice in some cases, but eventually surface soil found its way into them and is now the cause of crop marks. The appearance of these fossil frost cracks may vary considerably from place to place, but with experience they can be identified fairly easily in most cases.

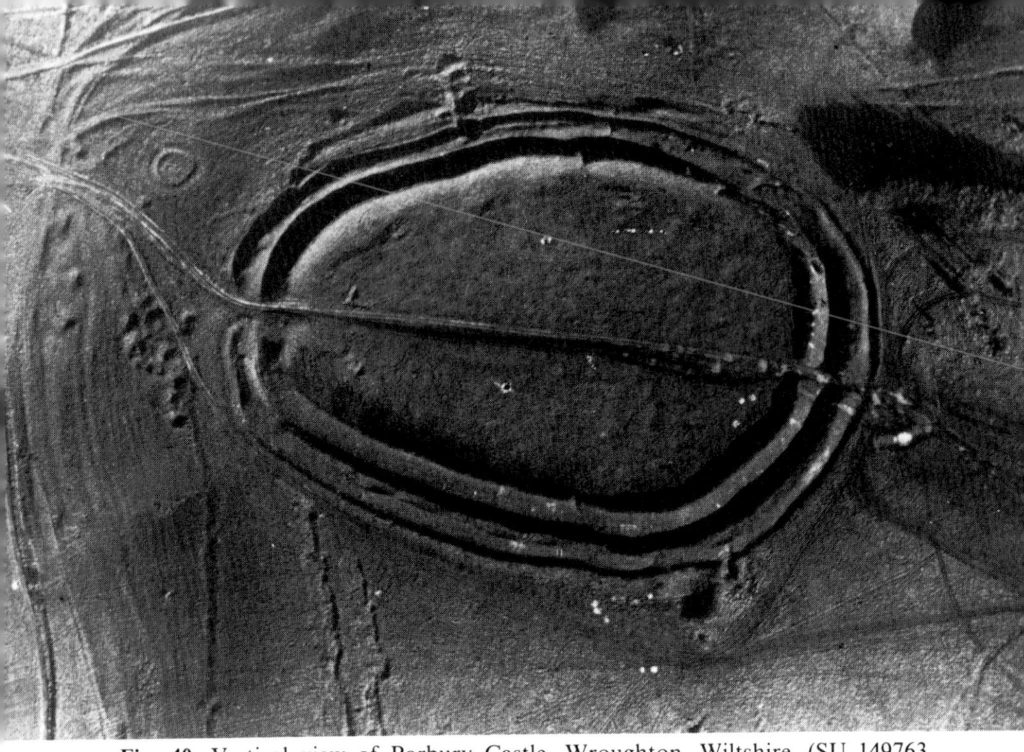

Fig. 40. Vertical view of Barbury Castle, Wroughton, Wiltshire. (SU 149763. 8.30 a.m. 22nd October 1943.)

Fig. 41. The Cessna 150 used by the author. A typical high-wing light aircraft.

6
Flying, photography and mapping

Equipment

In this book most of the photographs are oblique views taken by hand-held 35 mm or 70 mm cameras aimed through the cabin windows of light aircraft. This is the simplest form of photography, for which no modifications to the aircraft are needed. Oblique pictures present the view in a way which is easy to understand, but because of perspective distortion there are difficulties when it comes to preparing maps of the sites they show.

Vertical photographs show an unfamiliar direction of view (for example fig. 40, a view of Barbury Castle, on the Marlborough Downs), but mapping is more straightforward, though it must be remembered that these pictures are only completely free from distortion in their representation of the ground when it is flat and the aircraft was in a level attitude when the exposure was made. Verticals may be taken by means of simple installations in which a 35 mm or 70 mm camera of normal type is mounted in a light aircraft, either pointing through a small hole in the floor, or fixed to a frame projecting through a luggage hatch, or in a pod at the side of the fuselage. For accurate aerial mapping there are larger and more complicated installations incorporating special cameras which produce 230 mm square negatives, in which case a somewhat larger aircraft must be used.

Many different types of light aircraft may be employed. To minimise expense, the author, flying from the Sheffield Aero Club, makes use of the Cessna 150 and 152. These widely used models are high-wing single-engined monoplanes (fig. 41) which have a good field of view and are very convenient for oblique photography with hand-held cameras.

Taking oblique photographs from light aircraft

To produce obliques as well adapted as possible for subsequent use in mapping, the camera should be aimed at a steep angle downwards, and for this to be done the aircraft must be banked towards the camera side, which means that it will turn round the site being recorded. The direction of view of the camera should be at right angles to the flight path; pictures looking backwards or at queer angles should be avoided, though it is all too easy to take them to save time. It is necessary to include enough landmarks to provide fixed points for use in the mapping stage, and the picture should be composed in the camera viewfinder with this in mind – not always a simple matter, for example when a strong wind blows the aircraft either towards or away from the site. Flying at a suitable height helps to get the right area of land in the picture, and about 1500 feet (450 metres) above ground level is often a good compromise.

It is often necessary to select the right direction of view. Shadows generally show earthworks best when the observer is looking towards the sun, but if there is the slight haze which often accompanies clear weather in Britain visibility may be bad towards the sun, and the shadow photograph may have to be taken with the sun behind the camera; on occasions it is possible to compromise and take the picture looking across the sun's rays. Soil marks and crop marks are normally seen best looking with the sun, assuming that it is shining at the time, but there can be some strange effects with crop marks in cereals, particularly when they have grown tall and are still green (for example, fig. 20). It is often advisable to circle the site to find the best point of view, because marks in cereals may show well from one direction and almost disappear when viewed from another. A further point worthy of note is the advantage to be gained by taking shadow pictures of earthworks both in winter when the sun is low in the south and in summer when it is low in the east and the west; the two different views ensure that shadows reveal all the main features of a site.

Black and white photographs

The author does most work with black and white panchromatic film, used with the 2x yellow filter standard in the air for this type. This film reduces to a range of shades of grey the varying greens and browns by which most information about the surface of the earth is conveyed to the eye, so it cannot preserve the full range of information. Nevertheless, it provides an excellent record from which it is possible to obtain at moderate cost the large numbers of prints often needed to deal with the results of a single flight.

Panchromatic film has the advantage of considerable exposure latitude, so that a range of contrasts and light conditions can be accepted with the expectation of producing negatives from which good prints can be made. A fine-grained and relatively slow film (ASA rating about 100) can be used with advantage since there is usually plenty of light when air photographs are taken. There is then the question of making the archaeological information show well on the print or enlargement. The varying green shades in crops, which look rather striking from the air, may be difficult to record adequately in the greys of black and white film, and it is usually necessary to enhance their contrast. This may be done by under-exposing by one or even two stops, overdeveloping the negatives and printing on contrasty paper. On the other hand, shadow photographs of earthworks, including occasions when they are snow-covered, require normal exposure and development times as a rule. Dark-coloured bare soil may require a stop more than the figure indicated by the exposure meter.

Colour and infra-red photographs

Useful extra information can be obtained from the colour transparencies which are often taken to supplement black and white panchromatic pictures, but colour photographs have the disadvantages that they are not stable indefinitely and so are unsuitable as archive material, and also that prints are very expensive.

False colour infra-red film is an alternative supplement to black and white panchromatic. It is available in the form of transparencies, which show crop marks with extra contrast once the eye has become accustomed to their peculiar range of colours. The healthy plants forming the crop mark lines stand out well and false colour infra-red pictures can aid the interpretation of doubtful points. The use of black and white infra-red film has been advocated for shadow photography of earthworks, and it is useful on hazy days, but it introduces other problems and is not normally employed in light aircraft photography.

The stereoscope

A single air photograph can tell its user little about the height variations of the ground, which are difficult to appreciate unless they are emphasised by shadows, but a pair of overlapping pictures viewed through a stereoscope enables relief to be seen well. If an early site is to be understood, the hills and valleys of the adjacent countryside have to be taken into consideration, and the use of the stereoscope to assist interpretation is therefore important.

Mapping from vertical photographs

The production of maps from sets of overlapping photographs by photogrammetric means is now a highly developed process about which there is a large literature. Plotting machines, which may be of considerable size and complexity, can draw accurate maps showing the positions of surface features and height contours, provided that a specified number of points on the photograph have been surveyed accurately on the ground.

Vertical photographs may also be used as a source of detail to transfer to existing maps, a job which may with advantage be done on a sketchmaster, a simple piece of apparatus which is described in text books on air survey.

Mapping from oblique photographs

Most of the archaeological air photographs taken in Britain have been obliques. Good photographs of this kind may give excellent views of the sites they show, but they suffer from perspective distortion and their scales can vary widely according to the height at which the aircraft was flying, the focal length of the camera lens and the degree of enlargement of the print. The ancient remains shown by the photographs therefore cannot be fully understood unless maps are produced with distortion removed and the scale shown.

When remains such as ancient fields are to be studied, a large piece of ground has to be mapped, and maps of a scale of 1:10,000 or thereabouts provide a convenient base (for example, fig. 42). If the ground is reasonably flat, controlled sketching can give good results. There are various means of control, the simplest of which is to find a number of fixed points visible on both the map and the photograph and join them by lines which intersect the crop mark or other feature which is being plotted. There are other methods by which sketches can be controlled and reference may be made to a paper by J. N. Hampton in the reading list.

When preparing to map crop marks, there are often a number of photographs of the site extant. All should be consulted because, as explained earlier, the marks vary from year to year, and it is necessary to look at the pictures taken in several years to obtain the maximum amount of information. A single photograph, however good, is seldom enough.

The scale of 1:10,000 is too small when the details of some of the more important sites have to be plotted; in such cases 1:2,500 is often suitable (for example, fig. 43). The errors of controlled sketching here become magnified, and it is difficult to work to an acceptable standard. If suitable computer facilities are available (and the new microcomputers have enormously reduced equipment cost) an accurate map can be made by the recently introduced methods of removing perspective distortion and plotting by computer. Assuming again that the ground is reasonably level, a simple programme published by R. Palmer (see reading list) may be employed. Using a piece of apparatus described as a digitising table,

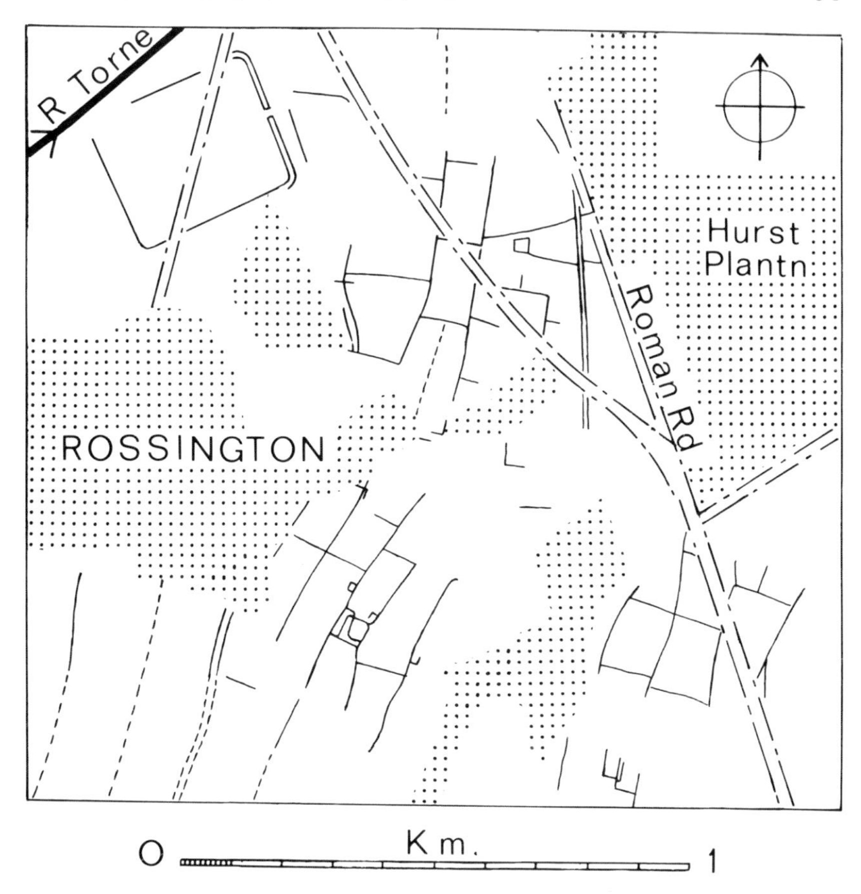

Fig. 42. Map of crop marks showing early fields, enclosures and a Roman vexillation fortress at Rossington, South Yorkshire. (Centre of map SK 632987.)

the positions of four control points identifiable on both the photograph and the map are fed into the computer. Then the crop mark lines or other ancient remains on the photograph are similarly fed in. The computer output takes the form of a drawing at the desired scale showing the four control points in their map positions and within them, correctly placed, a plot of the crop marks at the map scale and with perspective distortion removed. This can then be transferred to the finished map or drawing.

Two examples of maps of crop marks are given here. Fig. 42, which covers part of Rossington, South Yorkshire, was drawn at a

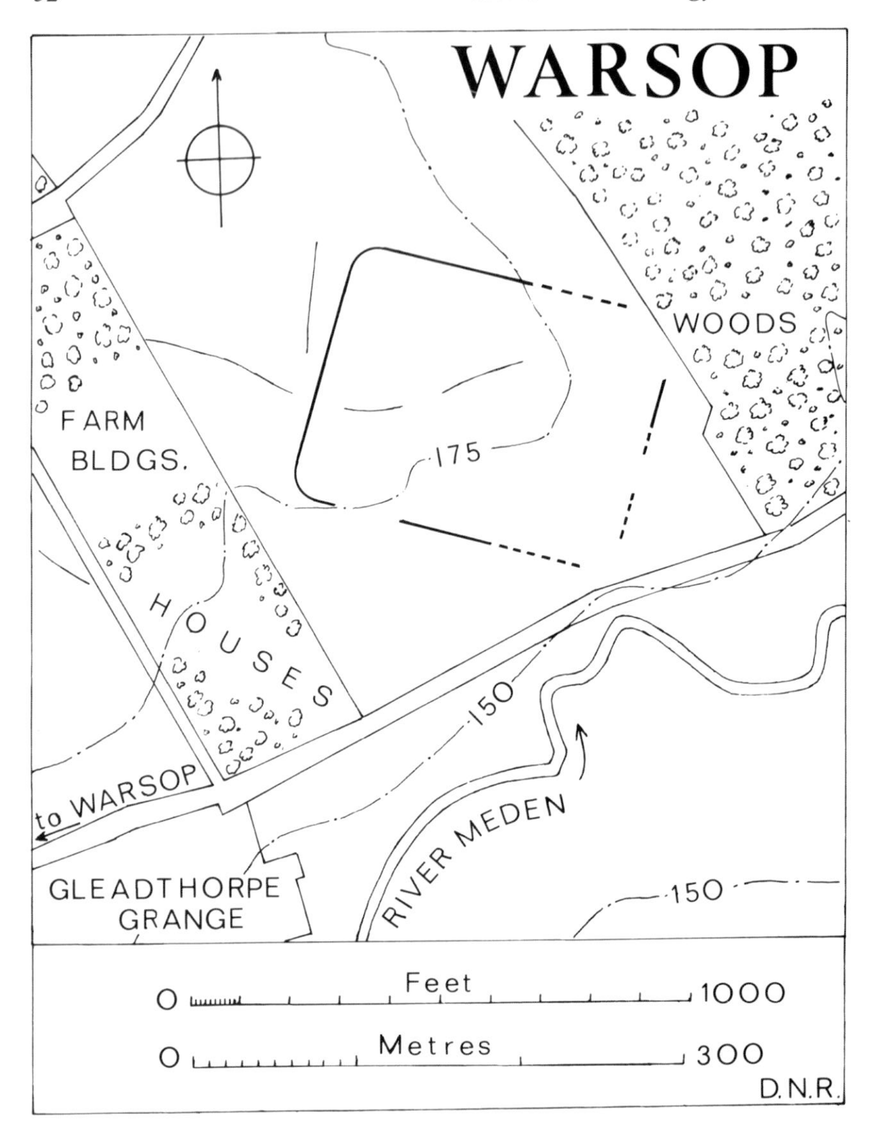

Fig. 43. Map of crop marks of a Roman marching camp at Warsop, Nottinghamshire. (SK 595704.)

scale of 1:10,000 and is here reproduced at 1:13,700. The crop marks are recorded by continuous lines where they are well established, and broken lines where doubtful. The modern boundaries are shown by chain-dotted lines. Areas in which crop marks cannot occur (built-up areas and woods) are stippled. The marks show a big system of fields, some enclosures and the Rossington vexillation fortress. Fig. 43 gives the Roman marching camp at Warsop, Nottinghamshire, drawn at 1:2,500 and here reproduced at 1:4,500. In this case the larger scale allows more detail to be included and different conventions are used for the modern features. There are many problems when attempting to reproduce on a map the complications recorded by air photographs, but space does not allow them to be mentioned here and reference may be made to a paper by Hampton and Palmer given in the reading list.

Taking air photographs of antiquities can be a rapid process when the aircraft has arrived over the site at the right moment. Completing the job by mapping the results is much slower and less exciting, but it is essential if full use is to be made of the results obtained in the air.

7
Further reading

BOOKS

Agache, R. *La Somme Pré-Romaine et Romaine.* 1978.
Benson, D. and Miles, D. *The Upper Thames Valley: An Archaeological Survey of the River Gravels.* 1974.
Beresford, M. W. and St Joseph, J. K. S. *Medieval England; An Aerial Survey* (second edition), 1979.
Bradford, J. *Ancient Landscapes.* 1957.
Crawford, O. G. S. and Keiller, A. *Wessex from the Air.* 1928.
Deuel, L. *Flights into Yesterday; the Story of Aerial Archaeology.* 1969.
Maxwell, G. S. (editor). CBA Report probably to be entitled *The Impact of Aerial Reconnaissance on Archaeology.* Forthcoming.
Phillips, C. W. (editor). *The Fenland in Roman Times.* 1970.
Riley, D. N. *Early Landscape from the Air; Studies of Crop Marks in South Yorkshire and North Nottinghamshire.* 1980.
Wilson, D. R. (editor). *Aerial Reconnaissance for Archaeology.* CBA Report number 12. 1975.

PAPERS

Early results

Akerman, J. Y. and Stone, S. 'Account of some Remarkable Circular Trenches . . . at Stanlake'. *Archaeologia*, 37 (1858), 1–8.
Downey, R. R. 'A History of Archaeological Air Photography in Great Britain'. *Orbit*, 1, 1980.

Surveys

Higham, N. J. and Jones, G. D. B. 'Frontiers, Forts and Farmers: Cumbrian Aerial Survey 1974–5.' *Archaeological Journal*, 132 (1975), 16–53.
Rhodes, P. R. 'The Celtic Field Systems on the Berkshire Downs.' *Oxoniensia*, 15 (1952), 1–28.
McCord, N. and Jobey, G. 'Notes on Air Reconnaissance in Northumberland and Durham' (two papers). *Archaeologia Aeliana*, 46 (1968), 51–67 and 49 (1971), 119–30.
Riley, D. N. 'Air Reconnaissance in Central and Southern Yorkshire in 1976.' *Yorkshire Archaeological Journal*, 49 (1977), 19–43.
St Joseph, J. K. S. Eight important papers on air reconnaissance in Roman Britain, covering work from 1945 to 1976. *Journal of Roman Studies*, 41 (1951), 52–65; 43 (1953), 81–97; 45 (1955), 82–91; 51 (1961), 119–35; 55 (1965), 74–89; 59 (1969), 104–28; 63 (1973), 214–46; 67 (1977), 125–61.
Webster, G. and Hobley, B. 'Aerial Reconnaissance over the Warwickshire Avon.' *Archaeological Journal*, 121 (1965), 1–22.

Reference may also be made to reports of current results in the journal *Aerial Archaeology*, 1 (1977), 2 (1978) and 4 (1979).

Papers on certain types of sites

Dymond, D. P. 'Ritual Monuments at Rudston, East Yorkshire.' *Proc. Prehistoric Society*, 32 (1966), 86–95.

Palmer, R. 'Interrupted Ditch Enclosures in Britain: the Use of Aerial Photography for Comparative Studies.' *Proc. Prehistoric Society*, 42 (1976), 161–86.

Wilson, D. R. 'Romano-British Villas from the Air.' *Britannia*, 5 (1974), 251–61.

Wilson, D. R. 'Pit Alignments: Distribution and Function.' In H. C. Bowen and P. J. Fowler (editors), *Early Land Allotment in the British Isles*, BAR 48 (1978), 3–5.

Techniques

Hampton, J. N., Palmer, R. *et al.* 'Implications of Aerial Photography for Archaeology.' *Archaeological Journal*, 134 (1977), 157–93.

Hampton, J. N. 'The Mapping and Analysis of Archaeological Evidence Provided by Air Photographs.' *Aerial Archaeology*, 2 (1978), 18–24.

Palmer, R. 'A Computer Method for Transcribing Information Graphically from Oblique Aerial Photographs to Maps.' *Journal of Archaeological Science*, 4 (1977), 283–90.

Riley, D. N. 'The Technique of Air Archaeology.' *Archaeological Journal*, 101 (1946), 1–16.

Index